Tuning In

Read the first couple of pages with the group to familiarise them with the way the information is presented. Then encourage the children to dip into the book and select the fish that they wish to read about. Support the children as they read, using the notes. Finish the session by drawing the group back together and asking the children what facts they have learnt.

The front cover

What is this encyclopedia about?

Will this book include common fish?

What do you notice about the way the title is written?

The back cover

What does the blurb tell us?

What sort of fish is this encyclopedia going to be about?

What do you notice about the way encyclopedias are organised?

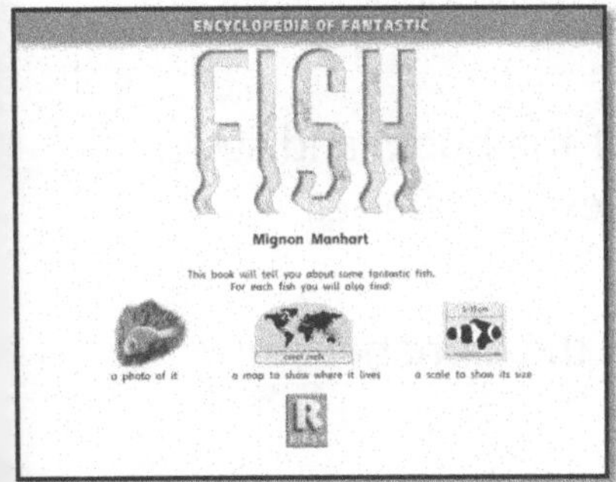

Contents

What three things will you find out about for each fish?

What does the map show? Why do you think part of the map is shaded?

READ

Read pages 2 and 3

Purpose: to investigate the structure of an encyclopedia.

EXPLORE

Pause at page 3

Look quickly through the book. What do you notice about the alphabet strip at the top of the page?

Now look back at the angler fish. What information are you given?

Let's look at page 3. Why does this page follow the angler fish? (*alphabetical order*)

READ

Read pages 4 and 5

Purpose: to use the glossary,

to use the alphabet to find your way around the encyclopedia.

EXPLORE

Pause at page 5

What is the title of page 4?

Find the words 'tentacles' and 'sea anemones'. Why are they in bold print?

Look at the glossary at the back of the book, and see what it tells you about the tentacles and the sea anemone.

Why is the letter 'D' picked out in the alphabet strip?

Angler Fish

The deep-sea angler fish uses a rod to fish for its dinner.

It is very dark in deep waters, so the angler fish has a light at the tip of its rod. When other fish see the light, they come close. Then the angler fish catches them!

Blind Catfish

Blind catfish live in dark caves. They have eyes, but they can't see. They use their whiskers to find food and to feel where they are going.

Clown Fish

Clown fish live between the **tentacles** of **sea anemones**. The tentacles contain poison, which protects the clown fish from **predators**.

Dwarf Goby

The dwarf goby is the size of a ladybird. It is the smallest fish in the world.

Tricky word (page 4):

The word 'anemones' may be beyond the children's word recognition skills. Tell this word to the children.

READ

Read pages 6 and 7

Purpose: to find facts about electric eels and frog fish.

EXPLORE

Pause at page 7

What happens if you touch an electric fence? What do you think would happen if you touched an electric eel?

Where do you find electric eels?

How do electric eels catch their prey?

Why does the frog fish have that name?

Where do frog fish live?

READ

Read pages 8 and 9

Purpose: to find out about grunt fish and hammerhead sharks.

EXPLORE

Pause at page 9

What do you think these fish are going to do?

Why are grunt fish sometimes called kissing fish?

What did you know about sharks before you read this? What new things have you learnt?

Why does this fish have such an odd-shaped head?

How big is this shark?

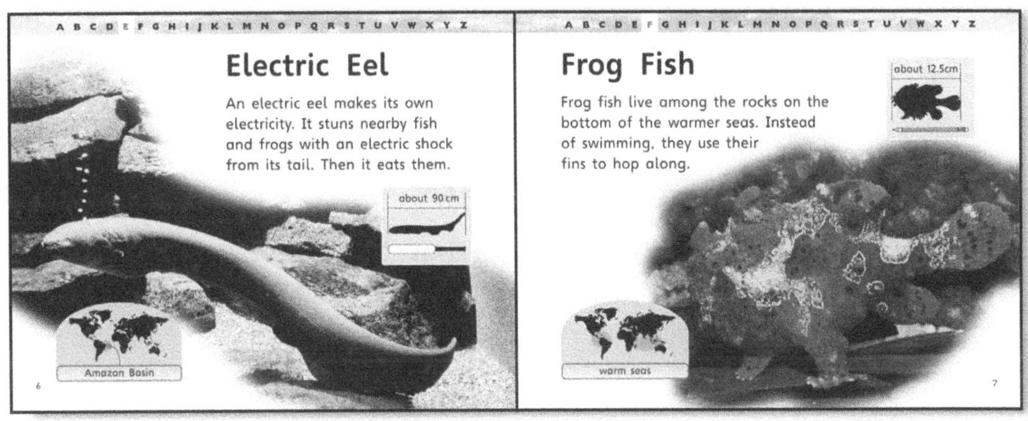

Electric Eel

An electric eel makes its own electricity. It stuns nearby fish and frogs with an electric shock from its tail. Then it eats them.

Frog Fish

Frog fish live among the rocks on the bottom of the warmer seas. Instead of swimming, they use their fins to hop along.

Grunt

A grunt grinds its teeth, making a sound like a pig. Two grunts may swim with their red mouths together. That is why they are also called kissing fish.

Hammerhead Shark

The hammerhead shark has an odd-shaped head. The hammer shape helps the shark to make sharp turns in the water.

5

Read page 10

Purpose: to find out how long a koi can live.

Pause at page 10

Look at the photograph. What different colours are the koi? (*orange, yellow, white, black, variegated*)

How long can they live for?

Where were they first bred?

Where do they live today?

Read page 11

Purpose: to discover why the fish is called a lantern fish.

Pause at page 11

Have you ever seen a picture of a lantern?

Why do you think this fish is called a lantern fish?

Where does the lantern fish have lights?

Where does it live?

How does it catch other smaller fish?

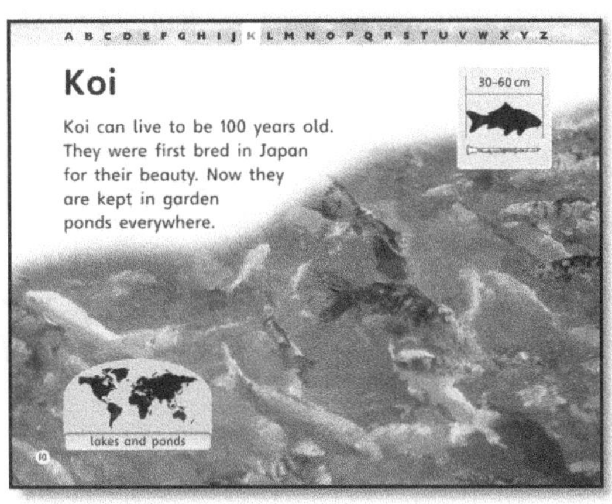

Koi

Koi can live to be 100 years old.
They were first bred in Japan
for their beauty. Now they
are kept in garden
ponds everywhere.

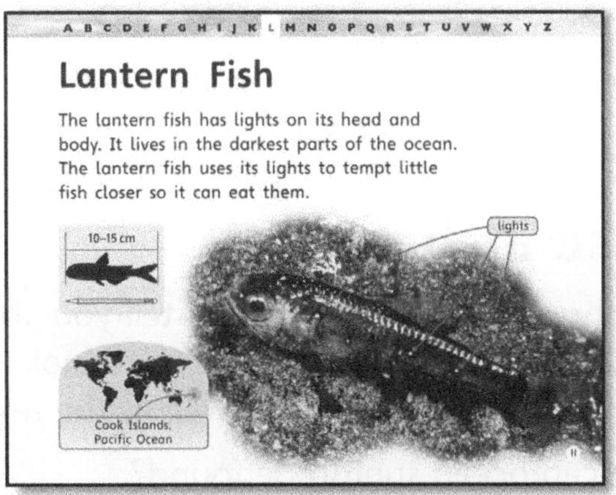

Lantern Fish

The lantern fish has lights on its head and
body. It lives in the darkest parts of the ocean.
The lantern fish uses its lights to tempt little
fish closer so it can eat them.

READ

Read pages 12 and 13

Purpose: to find out about lion fish and manta rays.

EXPLORE

Pause at page 13

Why do you think this fish is called a lion fish? (*because it is fierce. NB Lions do not have stripes!*)

How does the lion fish kill other fish?

Where are the fins on the lion fish?

Have you ever seen a ray in an aquarium?

What do the fins look like on the photograph?

Do manta rays look dangerous? What are they really like?

READ

Read pages 14 and 15

Purpose: to find out three things about the mudskipper and the sunfish.

EXPLORE

Pause at page 15

What three things does page 14 tell you about the mudskipper? (Remind the children to look at the photograph and diagrams as well as the text.)

Where can ocean sunfish be found?

Why is the fish called an ocean sunfish?

What other facts does this page tell you about the sunfish?

Lion Fish

The lion fish has fins that contain poison. The fins quickly kill a much bigger fish.

Manta Ray

The manta ray has fins that look like wings. Although it is big and looks fierce, the manta ray is gentle and graceful.

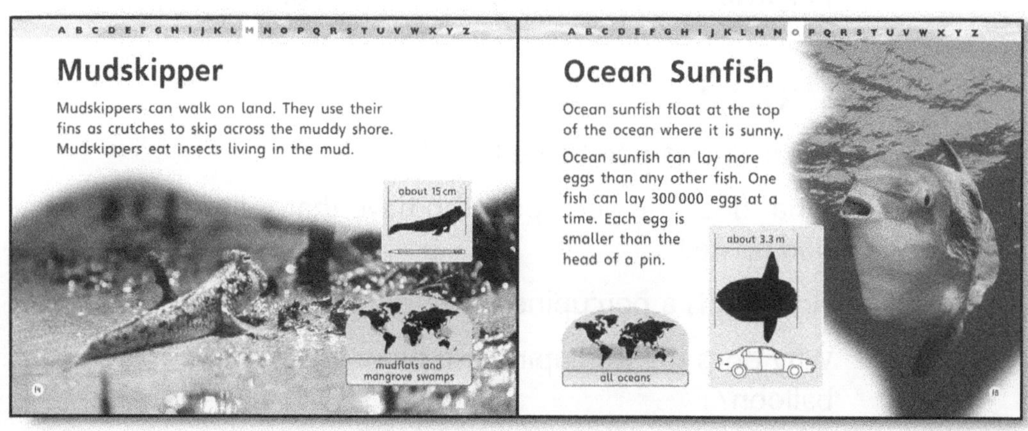

Mudskipper

Mudskippers can walk on land. They use their fins as crutches to skip across the muddy shore. Mudskippers eat insects living in the mud.

Ocean Sunfish

Ocean sunfish float at the top of the ocean where it is sunny.

Ocean sunfish can lay more eggs than any other fish. One fish can lay 300 000 eggs at a time. Each egg is smaller than the head of a pin.

READ

Read page 16

Purpose: to find out what piranhas eat.

EXPLORE

Pause at page 16

What makes you think this fish could be dangerous?

Where are piranhas found?

What do piranhas eat?

READ

Read page 17

Purpose: to find out about the spines of porcupine fish.

EXPLORE

Pause at page 17

What does a porcupine have?

What does the porcupine fish have that is like the porcupine?

How big is a porcupine fish?

Why does the porcupine fish blow itself up like a balloon?

What fact do you know about the spines on the porcupine fish?

Piranha

Piranhas have teeth like **razors**. They eat animals that live in rivers. Piranhas also eat fruit and seeds.

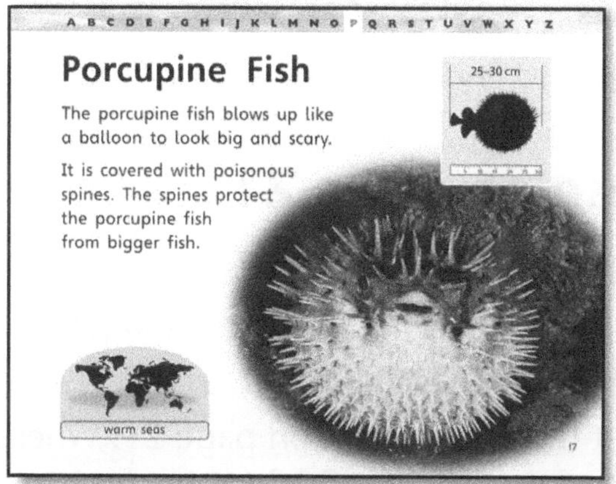

Porcupine Fish

The porcupine fish blows up like a balloon to look big and scary.

It is covered with poisonous spines. The spines protect the porcupine fish from bigger fish.

Tricky word (page 16):

The word 'piranha' may be beyond the children's word recognition skills. Tell this word to the children.

Tricky word (page 17):

The word 'poisonous' may also want to be discussed as a tricky word.

Read pages 18 and 19

Purpose: to pick out salient facts about the Russian sturgeon and the sailfish.

Pause at page 19

About how long is the Russian sturgeon?

What three facts have you learnt about it?

Look at the photograph on page 19. Why do you think this fish is called a 'sailfish'?

What land animal can move as fast as the sailfish? (*cheetahs – can run at 95kph*)

Read pages 20 and 21

Purpose: to find out about salmon and trumpet fish.

Pause at page 21

Have you ever eaten salmon?

Why do salmon swim upstream and jump up waterfalls? Are they strong swimmers?

Look at the photograph on page 21. Where is the mouth of the trumpet fish? (*at the bottom*)

Why do you think it is the same colour as the coral?

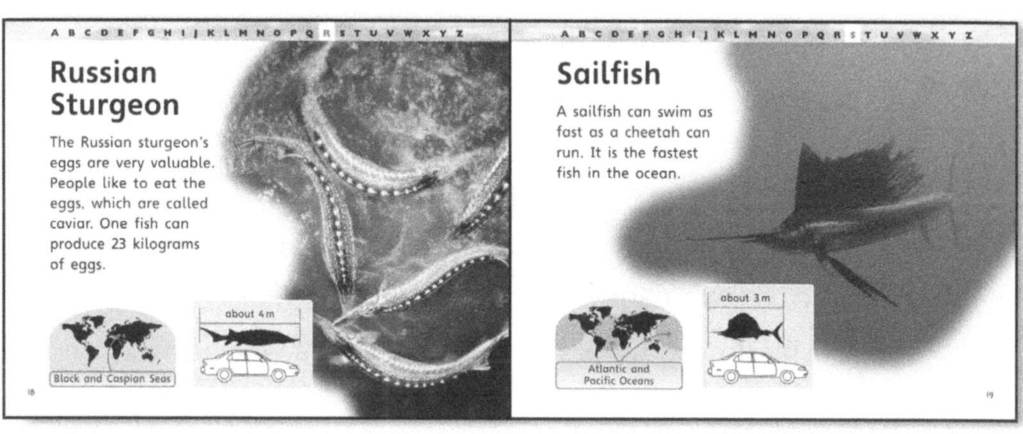

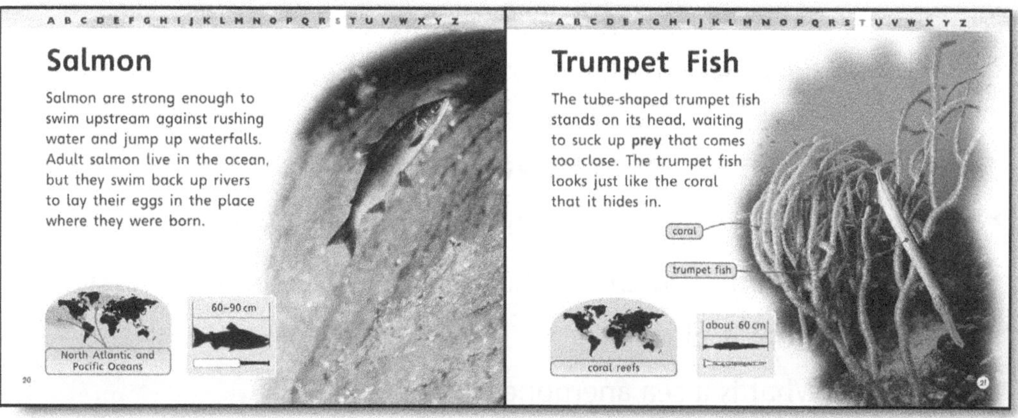

Tricky word (page 18):

The word 'sturgeon' may be beyond the children's word recognition skills. Tell this word to the children.

Tricky word (page 20):

The word 'salmon' may also want to be discussed as a tricky word.

READ

Read pages 22 and 23

Purpose: to find out about the whale shark's teeth.

EXPLORE

Pause at page 23

Look at the photograph. Why do you think it goes across two pages?

Why do you think this shark is called a whale shark?

How large is it?

How many teeth has a whale shark?

How does it get its food?

READ

Read page 24

Purpose: to use a glossary.

EXPLORE

Pause at page 24

Why do some non-fiction books have glossaries?

How do you know which words will be in the glossary?

What is plankton?

What is a sea anemone?

Whale Shark

The world's biggest fish has very small teeth. The whale shark has 300 rows of tiny teeth, which are useless for catching food. Instead, the whale shark uses gills like a net to scoop up **plankton**.

warm seas

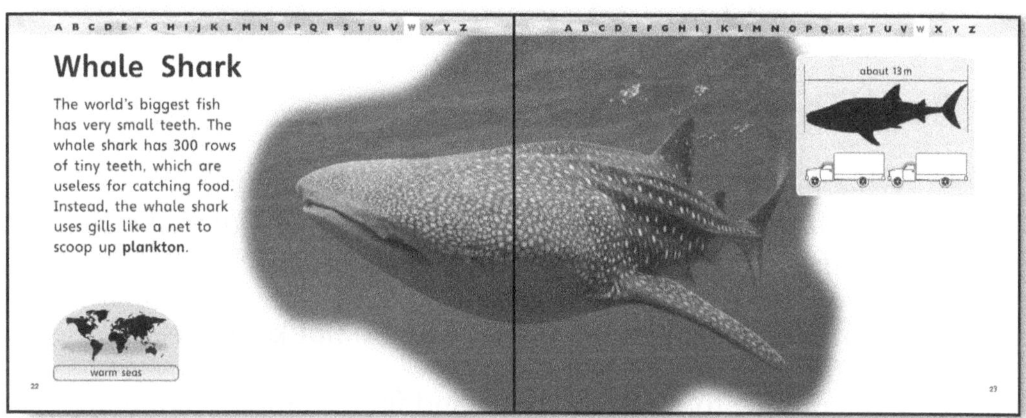

22

23

Glossary

plankton	tiny plants and animals that float in water
predator	an animal that hunts prey for food
prey	an animal hunted for food
razor	a very sharp cutting tool
sea anemone	a brightly coloured animal that looks like a flower, with tentacles around its mouth
tentacles	long flexible arms

24

After Reading
Revisit and Respond

- What features tell you that this is an encyclopedia? (*alphabetical order, contains similar facts about many different fish, uses diagrams, text, maps and photographs*)

- What facts have you learnt that you did not know before?

- Look quickly through the book and find examples of a map, a label, a scale that shows the relative size of a fish, and a glossary.

- Look through the book and find three examples of fish that have two words in their name (*e.g. catfish*). Write them down.